EXPLORE THE WORLD
PHYSICAL SCIENCE

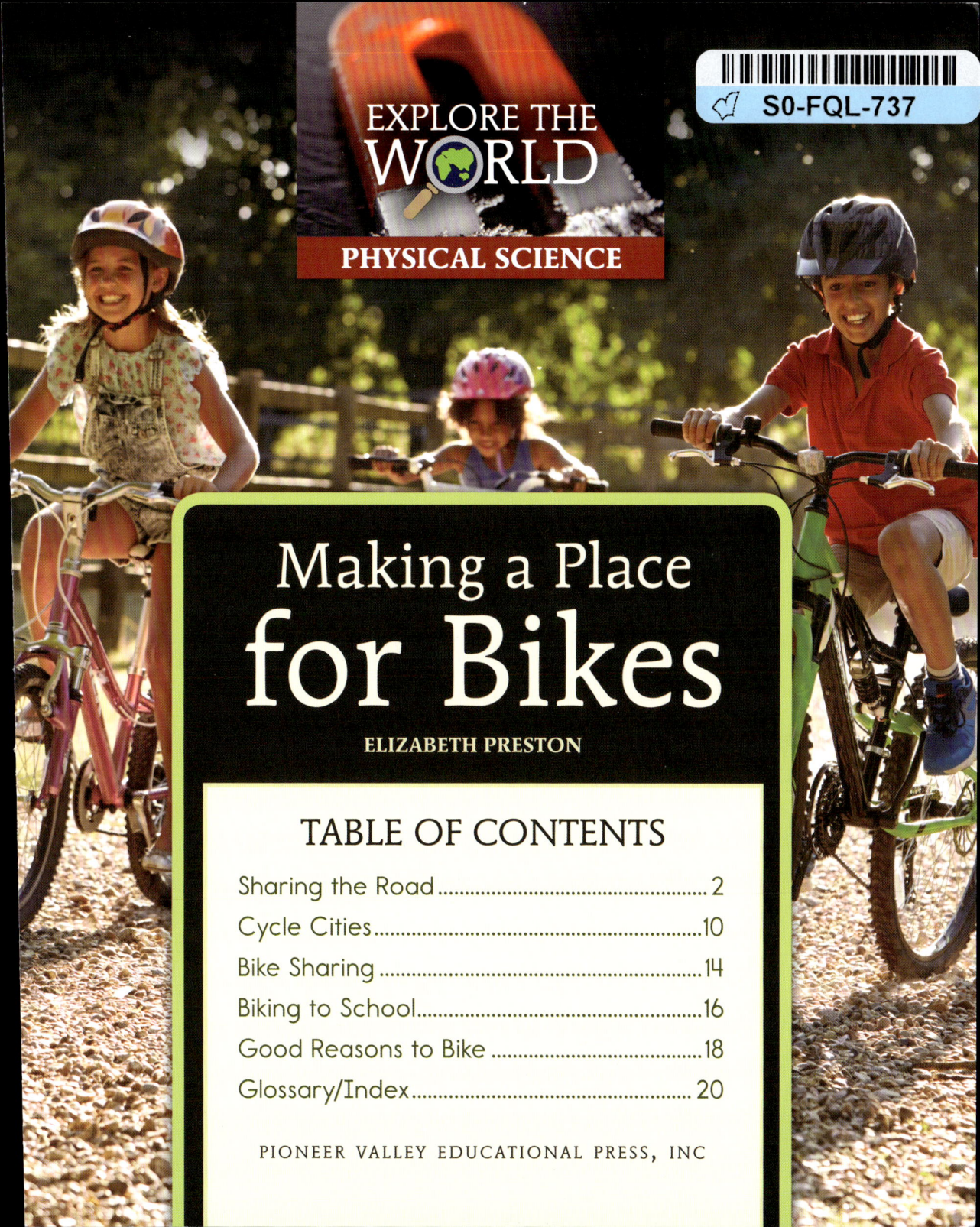

Making a Place for Bikes

ELIZABETH PRESTON

TABLE OF CONTENTS

Sharing the Road	2
Cycle Cities	10
Bike Sharing	14
Biking to School	16
Good Reasons to Bike	18
Glossary/Index	20

PIONEER VALLEY EDUCATIONAL PRESS, INC

SHARING THE ROAD

At first glance, bikes and cities may seem like a bad mix. There's so much traffic! Everyone is in such a hurry! Not to mention all those trucks and buses.

But for many city people, getting around by bike makes a lot of sense. Bikes are small, cheap, and easy to park. Biking is fun and good exercise. In cities around the world, more and more people are riding bikes—and cities are finding ways to help them share the road.

One of the simplest ways cities help **cyclists** is by making bike lanes. This is a traffic lane just for cyclists. Similar to lanes for cars, bike lanes are marked with painted lines. These **symbols** and colors say, "No cars allowed!"

Some cities put barriers between bike lanes and the rest of the road—a curb, a line of posts, or even a row of planters holding pretty flowers.

At **intersections,** a painted "bike box" helps bikers turn safely. Cyclists stop on the painted space to wait at a red light while cars wait behind them. Some bike lanes even have their own traffic lights.

5

The more bike-friendly a city becomes, the more people ride. In cities that build protected bike lanes, the number of people riding bikes often doubles.

MORE TO EXPLORE

BIKE MESSENGERS often deliver packages and newspapers. In some cities, even the garbage is picked up by bike.

Bike lanes can make traffic safer for everyone, not just cyclists. Cars slow down and drive more carefully next to bike lanes. When researchers watched videos of almost 13,000 riders in bike lanes at intersections in five big US cities, they didn't see a single accident. And when bikers have their own lanes, they don't ride on the sidewalk, so the people walking stay safer too.

Bike paths through parks or along trails can skip city streets altogether. In some places, old railroad tracks have been turned into paths for walking and biking. These **routes** were leveled out for trains, so once the rails are removed, they're perfect for bicycles. Sometimes you can ride these "rail trails" through cities and from one city to another.

>> The longest rail trail in the United States is in Missouri, and it is 240 miles long!

CYCLE CITIES

The Netherlands is a country where people really like bikes. Bike lanes are everywhere. So many people bike in the city of Amsterdam that they're running out of bike parking spaces!

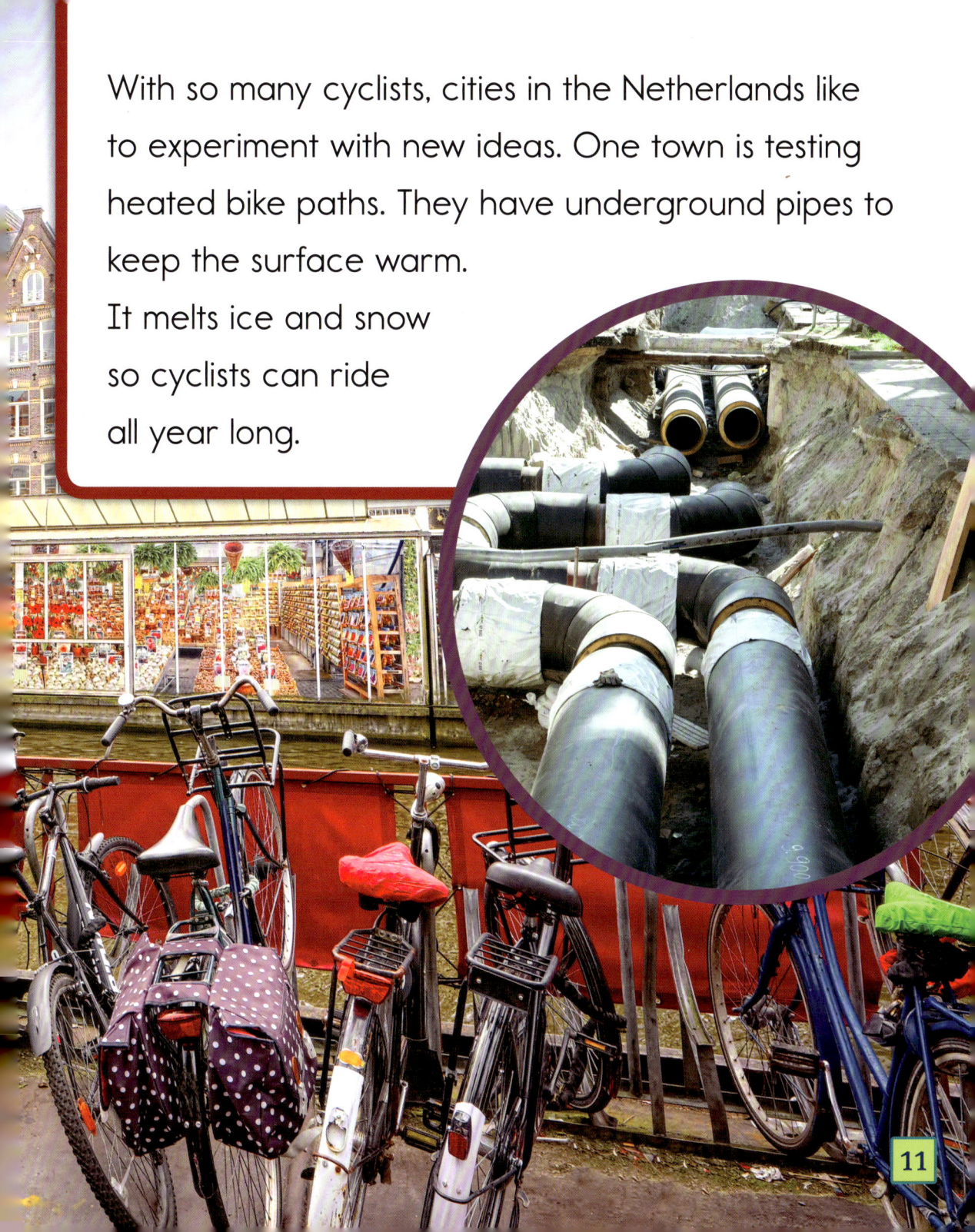

With so many cyclists, cities in the Netherlands like to experiment with new ideas. One town is testing heated bike paths. They have underground pipes to keep the surface warm. It melts ice and snow so cyclists can ride all year long.

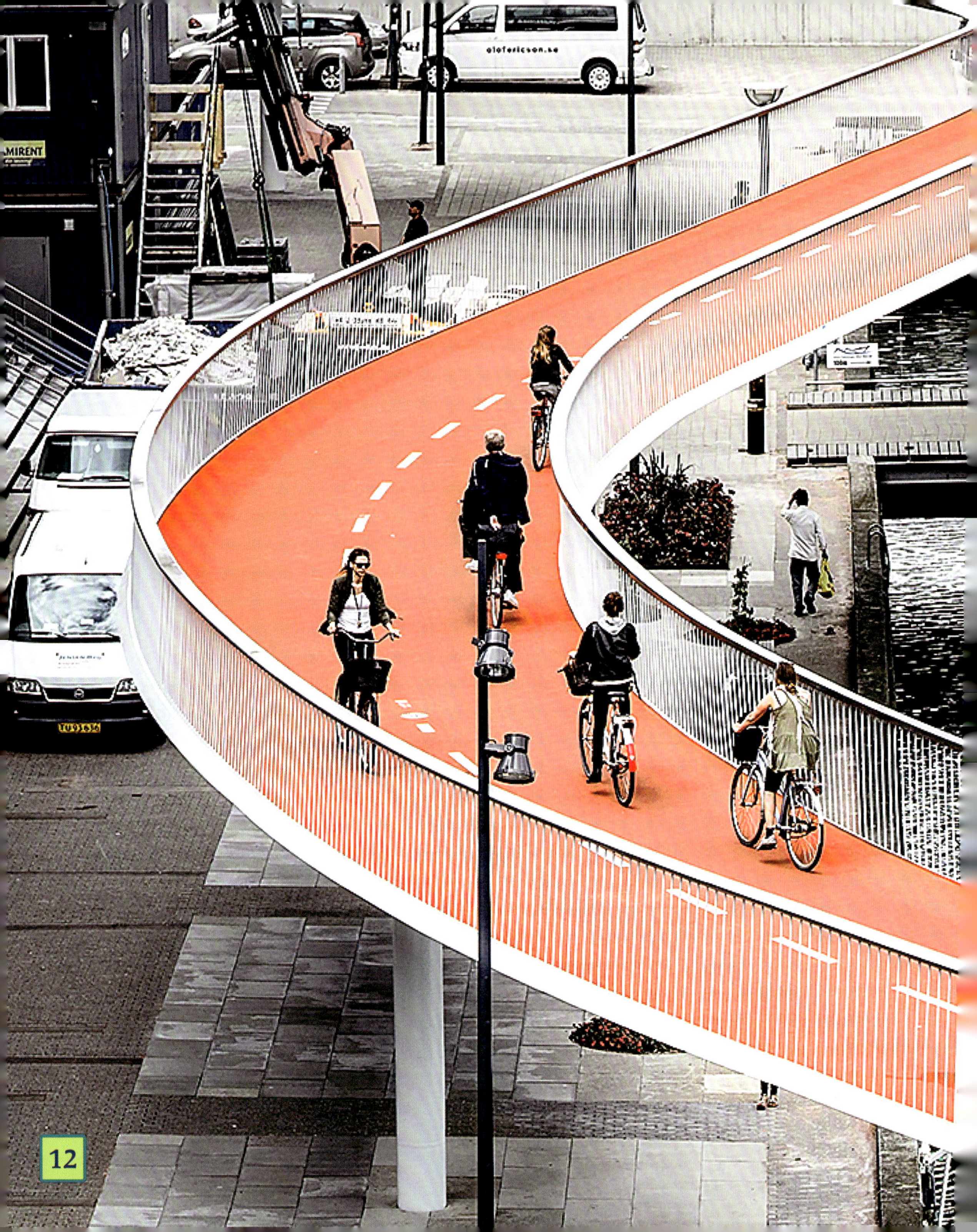
olofericson.se

Another bike-happy city is Copenhagen, Denmark. It has five times as many bikes as cars. To help all those bicyclists get across the harbor, a long, winding path that goes right over the water was built.

The path is called the Bicycle Snake. By separating bikes from other traffic, special paths like this make the streets less crowded.

BIKE SHARING

What if you don't own a bike or just want one for a day? Many cities around the world have bike-sharing programs, like lending libraries for bikes. In these cities, you'll see large groups of bikes lined up at sidewalk stations. For a small fee, you can check out a bicycle at one station, ride it, and leave the bike at a different station. This lets people cycle around without having to worry about buying, storing, or repairing their own bikes.

15

BIKING TO SCHOOL

For kids, bikes can also be a fun way to get to school. Some neighborhoods run bike trains. These are groups of kids who bike to school together with adults at the front and back of the group. The "train" stops to pick up more kids along its route.

In the Netherlands, kids ride actual bicycle buses. These specially made vehicles can seat 11 kids and 1 adult driver. Each rider has their own set of pedals. If the group's pedal power isn't enough to make it up a hill, an electric motor can give them a boost.

GOOD REASONS TO BIKE

There are many good reasons to like bikes. More bicycles on the roads mean there aren't as many people driving. This means less traffic and **pollution**. And that's good for the earth and all its people.

MORE TO EXPLORE

Bikes can help **POLICE OFFICERS** get into crowded areas that they couldn't get to in a car.

19

a pretty cky Mountains, ke paths. am allows at a bike

The streets of **New York City** can be extremely busy, and cycling is often the quickest way to get around. More than 200,000 city residents bike to work every day. The city also closes many of its parks to cars, making them easier to visit by bike.

Chicago has 200 miles of bike lanes, including some right on the street as well as some off-street. The city hopes to build three times as many bike lanes within the next few years.

Great US Biking Cities

Boulder, Colorado, town at the base of the Ro has hundreds of miles of b The city's bike-share progr users to pay by credit car station and go from there.

GLOSSARY

cyclists
people who ride or travel by bicycle

intersections
places where two or more streets meet or cross

pollution
substances that make land, water, air, and so on, dirty and unsafe or unsuitable to use

routes
ways to get from one place to another

symbols
pictures that are used instead of words

INDEX

Amsterdam 10
barriers 4
bicycle buses 17
Bicycle Snake 13
"bike box" 5
bike lanes 4–7, 10
bike messengers 6
bike paths 8, 11
bike-sharing programs 14
bike trains 16
Copenhagen, Denmark 13
cyclists 4–5, 7, 11
earth 18
garbage 6
harbor 13
intersections 5, 7
libraries 14
Missouri 9
motor 17
Netherlands 10–11, 17
pedals 17
pipes 11
police officers 18
pollution 18
"rail trails" 8–9
railroad tracks 8
researchers 7
routes 8, 16
sidewalk 7, 14
stations 14
traffic 2, 4–5, 7, 13, 18
United States 9